FELA ANIKULAPO-KUTI

THE PRIMARY MAN OF AN AFRICAN PERSONALITY

The Narrative & Screenplay

Introduction by Dr. Adetokunbo Ade-Banjo

Jawi Oladipo-Ola

FRONTPAGE MEDIA
OSOGBO - NIGERIA
2011

First Published 2011
© Jawi Oladipo-Ola & FRONTPAGE MEDIA 2011

Published by
FRONTPAGE MEDIA
19 BCGA Road (Top Floor),
Near Old Garage, Dugbe,
Osogbo, Osun State, Nigeria.
08034669598, 08055952722
E-mail:frontpagemediaosunnet@yahoo.com

Uk & USA Distributor
African Books Collective Ltd.
The Jam Factory, 27 Park End Street
P.O. Box 721
Oxford,0X1, 9EN, UK
Tel: +44(0)1865-726686
Fax:44(0)1865-793298
E-mail:orders@africanbookscollective.com
Website: www.africanbookscollective.com

ISBN 978-978-49986-3-5

Printed in the United Kingdom

Contents

All incidents and scenes in the
Screenplay took place in
its originality.
But the names could be
coincidental.

Acknowledgment

The historical perspective of Africa, from Fela Anikulapo-Kuti's point of view, is eye opening.

Our greatness is in the guiding principles of his music and politics. It is the path to Africa's future. Seeking first our political freedom, Fela's finds succor in Nkrumah's teachings that will nurture Africa, bring down every evil machination in its path to greatness.

Our ancestral spirit living in the minds of those fighting for a positive change are on the march now. It is good over evil. Africa is coming out.

In the fight of our lives, everyone, in our revolutionary spirit, is bound to overcome. When you no longer feel the excruciating pain of the evil forces, you are bathed in the force of blackism. That is the African personality, the grace of our home land. Africa, the source and origin.

I want to thank all those, who in their various capacity, keep resisting all forms of oppression, including those in Diaspora. We are getting there.

A big thanks to my brother and publisher, Bankole Ola. He has been part of the whole. He kept the light shining. I am proud of the collective doggedness, resilience and steadfastness in spite of all storms.

Thanks to Dr. Adetokunbo Ade-Banjo for writing an insightful and inspiring introduction to the book in spite of the short notice. And to my wife, Sumbo for being there. Victor, welcome aboard.

-Jawi Oladipo-Ola

Introduction

'Felabration' and 'Felasophy' are two new words I have heard since Fela Anikulapo-Kuti passed away in 1997. I was privileged to sit with Fela ten years before his death: it was an impromptu meeting after one of his nerve racking performances at the 'Shrine'. About ten young men of my age gathered around him to have a closer look, to hear him speak and draw inspiration. Regulars at the 'Shrine' will know that Fela always had one or two things to say after his shows.

As I was one of the closest to him, he looked at me, gave a smile and continued to talk to us. I could remember he advised us to help re-construct Africa and not to fall into the same category of our corrupt African leaders. He stressed further that Africa is the centre of the World and as the youths of the time we were the future and we should use whatever means to propel African unity and sustain her developments.

Invariably, Fela Anikulapo-Kuti was pitching 'Pan-Africanism' to us just like the pan- Africans before him, as the Narrative Section of this book rightly espouse. The Narrative Section also opens without reservation on 'Fela's philosophies on African development and solutions to the prevailing issues plaguing the process of development in terms of socio-political and economic restructuring.

Most Africa development strategists or analysts could have employed the services of Fela Anikulapo Kuti as his ideologies and philosophies would have fast-tracked the stagnant and unsustainable developmental ideas that have plagued the development process in Africa till date.

I cannot affirmatively attribute my current development disposition or ideas to Fela's mini speech in October 1986, but can confirm that Fela's ideas and philosophies were imbibed in my sustainable development theories for Africa. 'Felasophy' would in no time be adopted and used for Case Studies for development processes in less developed countries.

Empowerment is key to sustainable development. Fela empowered the world through his music and songs; he sang: 'Mr. Grammarticalization', 'Teacher Don't Teach Me Nonsense', 'Coffin for Head of State', "International Thief Thief' the list is unending. These songs are prime examples of Fela's education to Africans and the world at large. A wake up call to reality as the majority were being short changed by the few at elm of affairs.

Fela sang against SAP (Structural Adjustment Programme: Introduced by IMF, supposedly to accelerate sustainable development in less developed countries) long before the loan was taken up by the Nigerian government at the detriment of over 100million people in Nigeria.

As an advocate of sustainable rural development, I strongly identify with Fela's resolve that for development to be effective and sustainable, it has to be people-centred, not only in the sense that the people are the beneficiaries for development (Speth 1993), but also, and perhaps more importantly, in the sense that development is undertaken by the people for the people.

Apparently, Fela did not in the least benefit from his advocacies, but had stationed strong legacies in the minds of many Africans and other people from less developed countries. His songs and numerous symposia are testaments to this.

In the eighties he carried mock coffin to the Dodan Barracks, Lagos, the Nigeria power sit, equivalent of The White House and Downing Street at Whitehall London, to demonstrate and protest the death of innocent African citizens and especially his mother (the first Nigerian woman to drive a car in Nigeria) due to government mismanagement and collapse of law and order in most Nigeria cities.

Fela Anikulapo-Kuti: The Primary Man of An African Personality by Jawi Oladipo-Ola is another insight into Fela's lifestyle and personality, with emphasis on his Pan-African beliefs. The distinguishing factor is the fact that the book is written as a narrative and screenplay, a rare styled book on Fela in recent years. This book will surely influence the minds. It is profoundly narrated, yet intensely structured to strengthen the effect of Fela Anikulapo-Kuti's philosophy of life and development processes.

The Narrative Section begins with comparative philosophies of various African leaders, like: Thomas Sankara, Lumumba, Senghor, Nkrumah and others. With these great Pan-Africans its Fela Anikulapo-Kuti on the plaque.

My emphasis are on the uniqueness of style and make believe life-like narrative techniques of Jawi Oladipo-Ola in the book. The captivating effects of Fela ideas in his words in the

Screenplay Section and the switch from Queens English to pidgin English show cased the originality of the book and true representation of 'Felasohpy' and what Fela truly stood for.

The screen play provides sufficient materials for any good movie on the legend.

Dr. Adetokunbo Ade-Banjo
United Kingdom

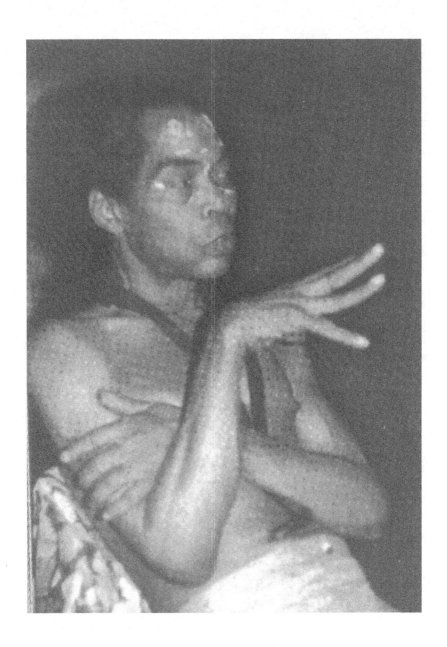

THE NARRATIVE

The greatest African that lived in modern times since Kwame Nkrumah, Sekou Toure, Lumumba, Nasser, Sankara, Senghor, Benbella is FELA ANIKULAPO-KUTI. Kwame Nkrumah and Malcolm X had the greatest influence on his political philosophy: Africa Will Unite. Marcus Garvey started this political thought flow. Where Awolowo, Kenyatta and Nyerere lived for African Unity, Nnamdi Azikiwe ceremoniously pursued this political philosophy and African nationalism.

Fela is a man who discovered himself and defined his own identity. Practical and pragmatic, Fela, legendary in his political firebrand music, created his own value system. Fela would like to be seen as an ethnomusicologist, pantheist and Africanist. He felt for Africa's future. He felt for the glorious past of great Africans and their contributions to the world.

Fela's greatest creation was himself, evolving into an African Personality. He won and mastered his own desires and the understanding of the creative use of those powers. By overcoming himself, he overcame all his adversaries.

Marcus Garvey, Patrice Lumumba, Malcolm X and Kwame Nkrumah were Fela's men of action whose theories were his

1

building principles. This historical perspective revealed Fela's might.

Their line of thoughts, researches and actions were formulated from our historical experience, the principle of the African Personality and Pan Africanism. Fela's resolution is the dissolution of the surface life in Africa. His determination is the emancipation for Africa and the blackman's plight.

Fela was a fearless critic of vanity and bad faith with great knowledge and understanding of the society he lived in. Fela's moral standard is guaranteed by the light of his own virtue, a synergy prevalent in his music and politics, the value system of a categorical Pan Africanist.

Fela Anikulapo-Kuti, Marcus Garvey, Patrice Lumumba, Malcolm X and Kwame Nkrumah have one burning desire, one goal; the salvation of black people all over the world and the total liberation of the black world from oppression and subservient dependence.

The emergence of the black experience, framework of thinking and action, the product of our collective historical experience can only come from a united effort undertaken by an Africanist of Fela's magnitude. He arrived at this conclusion from his own assessment and analysis of the African situation. The wisdom of his argument is not only in his music, it is the exemplary character of his belief.

Primarily, Fela embraced and promoted African belief, institution, desires and the ingenuity of African culture and tradition with the equal passion of his music. The spirit of Fela's music is the essence of the big difference in human culture and thought, between rational and aesthetic experience. Fela's ingenuity is his universal attempt to express the African personality.

Fela has an unpleasant and dangerous qualifier for Islam and Christianity. To him, Christianity is more of a song and poetic dance conceit. Islam is in a lesser context. He critically questions Christian and Islamic principles, especially its colonization that changed the social evolution and complexion of the traditional African value system. Africa's rich human value system evolved from a powerful hierarchy formed on the spiritual traditional principle of Africans. Fela promoted these ideals with the zeal he put into his music.

WHEN THEY CAME THEY GAVE US THE BIBLE. WHILE WE SHUT OUR EYES LOOKING UP TO GOD IN HEAVENS, THEY STOLE OUR LAND -Bishop Desmond Tutu

The concepts, images and feelings of Fela's politics became dominant under the influence of his music. His music invites us to symbols and feelings of the African, emphasizing the images of the African Personality. Fela promoted, that there will be fusion progression, an attitude, that will absorb useful qualities of every culture. That is, when other cultures meet the African Personality, the blend will bring goodwill to Africa.

Fela is spokesman and ambassador of Africa. His admirers called him the "Black President" as an advocate for African Unity. His only pain is the horrors, degrading disorders and pollution of the continent by the elites. It depresses him so. His greatest disappointment is the chaotic difference in Africa and the suffering in the land. He has bitter disgust for Africans who work with non-Africans against the blackman. Today, the continent has lost its traditional value because of the socio-economic politics not rooted to an African ideology. For Fela, Pan Africanism is the option, Africa was his vision. He was very passionate for Africa. Fela see modern African culture as sick. To him, African traditional culture must be revived to achieve greatness.

FOR A WAY OUT, WE ARE NOT LOOKING EAST OR WEST, WE ARE LOOKING FORWARD-Kwame Nkrumah

Fela Anikulapo-Kuti's music led us to the Pan African perception of seeing the world. His music is African spirituals in his own value system. While he forces us to gaze into the horrors of the individual, as an individualist, Fela pulls down the whited sepulcher of our religiosity and beliefs. Yet he carries everyone along his voyage of African consciousness, BLACKISM: a force of the mind. He believes we should take from the past to make a new life and culture. Through Fela's music, we can face the good ideas of Pan Africanism and the message of Nkrumah. To achieve this aim, Fela used argument.

PAN AFRICANISM IS THE ANSWER! The question is that African culture will lead us to Fela's messages to Africans and African descent. Fela's repertoires are the value in human lives, to him, African life is the greatest culture: our genuine anthropology.

4

Fela, an evolved man, primarily committed to the emancipation of Africa has a total disregard for military governments whose culture is corruption. He has no respect for military governments, who in their jingoism are a danger to African culture. They still remain a threat to Africa by idealizing a military group that has lost its spartan qualities. Every military government extorted the African people who merely emulated their irrelevances and corrupt nature. The most important event that shaped Fela's ideas was the Nigerian civil war.

Fela connects the African Personality ideals to the common man who ask very little of life. Fela sees the contempt African elites have for the people who he exploits and oppress. He does not miss the point to accuse the elites of inhumanity and corruption. When Fela became the problem to issues, he will not conform his style to rational expressions. He rattled the elites with caustic language and jeered at their excesses.

Fela's political discretion comes first, followed by the ideological poetic ideals. His politics was the means to his compositions. He despise the elites who treat him as a denigrate and corrupted youths. They say he demonizes the youth. Fela mocks conventional morality and taunts frivolous contents in no solemn tone but in his vulgarized chants. The conventional wisdom he turns into farcical comedy irritates the elites and leaders.

To Fela, African leaders are graven images and tragic heroes. They abused and operated wrong systems. Fela's interest is the battle for Africa's survival. You experience the African tragedy as a stage play in his functional music without losing the form. The function of his music is the basic comparison to the concept of the

African Personality: Africa overcoming its weakness in pursuit and quest for greatness.

Fela is the great bridge to Pan Africanism and the African Personality. He goes across and gets on the spirituality of the African continent with his highly technical and detailed music. The libidinous passion of Fela's music is an art in applied science and life affirming human factor and condition. Fela is never a moralist in the history of morals.

Fela's sexuality is his attempt to seek a path back to the womb, a voyage from the prison of this bitch of a life. The labial consonant in his music adds to the sensual image of Fela.

Fela is not bohemian. He is a liberal hedonist who celebrates perpetual youth without being exuberant. He glorified his own virtues. He was a non conformist, an unrepentant renegade but he has a cause: African Unity.

What makes the African Personality? Africanism is the affirmation, an affirmative action of the personality, the identity and the richness of the African way of life.

The African society is communal. It embraces individual growth towards a group welfare. An African society, which seeks the well being of the community in the context and welfare of the group, will defeat colonial mentality. Fela's will to fight political subjugation, economic exploitation, educational and social backwardness propels the functions of his music.

To reconstruct that traditional Africa society, the African human value system must be reinvented. The concepts of Africanism have that essential socio-political and ideological connotation.

WE MUST DARE TO INVENT THE FUTURE- *Thomas Sankara*

Fela's philosophy of Pan Africanism is his commitment to the total liberation of Africa and a union of African state government, for economic unification beginning with the black consciousness struggle for emancipation from the diasporas. When Fela's music changes to a more political tone, he sought mass participation; "Mobilization Against Second Slavery", to protest the privatization and globalization of the African economy.

The Fela communiqué was that Africa must emerge from this savage condition called civilization, back to the traditional model, the essential African model of community self government within our native intelligence. The Nigerian state mechanism constantly crucified Fela for promoting new values on new law tables. They sacrificed his future to themselves. African leaders mutilated the continent and scrambled for the spoils of the nation states.

Fela admonished that there is value in what the past can say about the African governing system. African elites failed to recognized and appreciate these models of the African society. They came to build their own eurocentric model structure, which has failed till today. That is why Africa has a pauper economy, believing that Africans do not have an enterprise economy. Though Fela despises utopia, to him it is catastrophic, it is bad for

7

creativity and human life.

Africa has reached the peak of degradation; it is now on the path of greatness and achievement. Africans are increasingly disengaging themselves from their national economy that abused and oppressed them. This is a disengagement from the state to escape excessive oppression by the elites whose political science does not teach African history. The nationalism of the elites and their patriotism is a refuge. These scoundrels created a militarized government that leaves destruction on its path with no developmental value. But the path to greatness has begun from the creativity and dynamics of black people all over the world.

Africa will be free from its present nation state; its peak ready to collapse because past African governments have been disastrous with massive oppressive corruption and subservient to foreign manipulations. Black nations have always facilitated foreign government in exploiting Africa. "Something of our own" is a significant distinguished message in Fela musicology of the African Personality.

Fela's personal spiritual convictions overshadowed his global political preoccupation. His personal integrity and loyalty to Africa is a result of the experience and information he has. His religiosity played a role in determining his political orientation of a purely African Personality, which to him is spiritual. Fela assumed and instills these responsibilities in his repertoires.

Blackism, a force of the mind is economic power. It heralds the long awaited buy MADE IN AFRICA: 'BUY AFRICA', an economic liberation struggle from colonial mentality and the shadows of obscurity with goodwill to everyone. To understand Fela's music you must live it. His music is unity song. The joy and sorrows, love and hatred, the hope and despair of Africa move the people to the direction of total liberation. Fela's music is functional in a communal context, style, definition and movement.

Fela's music is his own experience and thoughts. He lived it. He articulates the separateness of the African. His artistic rebellion against western cultures is a rejection of the American and European cultural values while impacting the African Personality. The music of Fela is a vehicle to economic development. His music is a charismatic effort to rally support for the African Personality that promotes the economic and social development of Africa. Fela's consistent Africanist dimension of his music emphasizes black internationalism. Africa is a political economy that has always attracted non-African for economic and investment opportunities. This is closely associated with African anthropology.

The African Personality of Fela is on higher ground, a reconciled form of the society where every thing works, where the ordinary African asserts himself within the modern complexities of globalization. Fela, coming from the past, has a vision of a greater African society, a new African society that must absorb positive contributions of great Africans. The social dimension of his political music is the rejection of the label- "Third World"-in his song for international acceptance. Human right replaced local political view with the international understanding of world geo-political economy.

In what relation does Fela's music stand to the image and concept of Pan Africanism? Fela's music is a vehicle for development, a means of communicating idea, vision and information to the people towards achieving national development and personal growth. It is basically to mobilize the people for socio-political awareness. The primary aim is self-development, actualization and empowerment.

Fela's faithfuls at the Shrine and his Kalakuta home are not cultic. At any given time, they put away language and personal identity to enter the Felaic music with ecstatic dance and intoxication, which is a means. The mythical collectivity of Pan Africanism is the end.

The Fela's African Shrine is ritual theatre. It is an all participatory. The audience and performers are indivisible where Fela, without any hint, is always in control of his emotion, giving no hint of his personal insecurities. The driving force is his passion for Africa.

His effort to defend Africa is obvious in his music. He parades and asserts himself with pride and style. For the fact, that before the telescope, the Dogon tribe of Mali have knowledge about an obscure invisible star. Fela strongly believe that there is a fraud in the general information about Africa. All available evidence on Africa before European colonization shows that there was an advanced growth and development, a well-organized society in Africa.

Fela's African Personality is the smooth road to economic development; an effort to support the policies that will promote economic regional development. There must be a return to the "status quo ante" the communal value system; where we must look out for each other. We must re-read the continent's history. There is motivation in it. Long before colonization, Africa boasted strong prosperous empires. Fela believed in a new Africa for spiritual balance, social regeneration, mental and a political union. His music punctures every fabric of our mediocrity. Defiance was always part of Fela's public attitude. His personality endures through his life than most of his songs.

If Fela's personality outlasted most of his songs, it is a personality intimately connected with his compositions and arrangements. He expresses himself best and most characteristically in a resourceful musical spirit.

Fela's true sense wiseness is his lifelong assault on common-place life and common sense values. It is a common knowledge that the conventional world struck at Fela, his character, his ideas and philosophy. His several arrests, harassments, imprisonments, detentions were the effect of his cause and beliefs.

In his own analysis, Fela's music is not Afrobeat. It is erotic theatre, exotic, intelligent and sensitive. It is not dance hall music. It is a political statement, call and response with an emotional climax in a polyrhythm lead beat. It is this richness of Fela political music, his sharp insight and foresight, that confused the elites and oppressive governments. The soul of Fela's music is the cultural history of Africans striving for humanity in a world of oppression.

Essentially, his music is a social commentary of the consciousness and the dehumanization of Africa and the Blackman.

11

He sees political parties of the elites as a grim enterprise that involves the slimmest vulgarity of man against man. The rejective Fela is the significance of the political philosophy, action, hedonistic, sacrificial and sensual life he lived.

Fela's consistent militant dimension in his music emphasized black internationalism, not as an end in itself, but as a means towards accomplishing one of the most basic needs for Africa's future. His music is of an unhappy people, disappointed and oppressed, seeking a free world, pursuing the good life.
He knew the role of black people in history. He saw the importance of linking black people all over the world with his struggle for a greater Africa. Fela stressed the international character of the Blackman's struggle, oppression, exploitation and destiny in the African Personality.

Fela's proposition is in concert with Malcom X concept of continental alignment of black people as the only possible black consciousness perspective. Fela promoted African emancipation and black consciencism by increasing awareness and identification of Africa, African culture and values of "OUR OWN". Fela was an internationalist, who understood the role Africans played in history.

His philosophy is the ideological framework and thought patterned to the experience and needs of Africa and Africans.

If not for his music, the beginning of Fela's music career was conducive to individualism. He was an individualist.

Contemplative Fela keeps his ideals pure in the purest form of art and the man affirming the meaningfulness of the African Personality.

The wisdom of his argument is not only in his music, it is the exemplary character of his virtuos beliefs. Fela's revel actions, led him into more understandings towards a more agitated action. He was not only occupied with the black man's experience, he wanted to emancipate. Fela promoted the African personality, the renascent of Africanism as a relevant ideology of blackism. Fela's love for Africa is that of historical experience common to black people all over the world. Fela is the last man to have the ingenius qualities of an African personality. His universal ingenuity is an expression of the African personality proper.

Fela, having studied, researched, analyzed the blackman's dilemma and everything that could change the plight of the blackman on his own, tried to get to the root of our reality. He sought answers and solutions that corresponded to our own historical experience.

Fela ANIKULAPO-KUTI had one primary aspiration: the evolution of a new black race, a new black civilization and, a new black destiny. Fela gave and instilled a sense of racial, cultural and historical pride. Fela gave us self-confidence and courage. He confronted us with our responsibilities. He pursued the historical vision for constructing an independent future. He created awareness; created new knowledge of self-determination, identification, and definitions.

Fela neither shrank in the face of tyranny, nor compromised the destiny of the black man. He fought his adversaries as a full man. Fela's life wrote his music and his greatness wrote his life.

AFRICA WILL WRITE HER OWN HISTORY. AND IT WILL BE A GLORIOUS AND DIGNIFIED HISTORY
-Patrice Lumumba.

Fela Anikulapo-Kuti fought for a *F*ree, *E*mancipated and *L*iberated *A*frica. He was a cure to our diseased society. And we're all part of that society. Fela was betrayed by the moral stupidity of a sick and dangerous country.

FELA... For Ever Lives Africa!

JAWI OLADIPO - OLA

THE SCREENPLAY

SCENE 1, ACT 1

EXTERIOR BARBER SHOP- DAY

A Whiteman is seated in barber seat wrapped in white barber cloth. Barber clips away at Caucasian hair.
Shot close in on spread newspaper. Cigarette smoke coming from behind.
Newspaper headline: Housing for all. New development plan approved. Uniformed soldier await turn, propped on rifle. A picture of Federal and Biafran soldiers embracing, at end of civil war. Music "Viva Nigeria" of Fela.

SHOT BACK AT BARBER

BARBER

Di time wey Issac Boro dey talk say 'ojoro' dey who fit talk dat time. Only im say, im no go gree, (music: no agreement)

Shot at newspaper closing, showing man with dangling cigarette from his mouth.

MAN

That was a great Nigerian, too. Kaduna Nzeogwu.
He saw everything. All the lies and deception going on then.
Now it is time to bamboozle us with housing scams.
This country is a hoax. Ojukwu had to put up a fight. In the process, it triggered a looting spree.

Shot back at barber

BARBER

Ojikwu see all the lie-lie, wuruwuru.
With all our independence; what do we have? Dem just dey fuck our yansh anyhow. But one-day monkey go market. He no go return. Naim be say, monkey eye don open. Baboon go vex; when monkey refused to work

> *Shot on a little girl from barber's shop, Opens door, thrust basket bag through door opening. Manage to go through door without upsetting basket contents.*

16

BARBER

Hey, Titi, where is your mother?
You only brought in the drinks
*Girl wade through shop . Set bottles of home
made local bootleg 'Ogogoro'*

As he clips and trims bottle clangs is heard

BARBER

Careful with those bottles if you don't
want your mother to konk your head. I
go first sama your face for here. *Door
opens. Uniformed soldier comes in with
rifle strapped on shoulder. A hand
grenade hooked to waist. All dressed up
in camouflage.*

BARBER

Officer, you don't come. You meet us well. You are just on time.
The drinks just came. Serve yourself as usual.

Goes to "bar" to dispense himself.

SOLDIER

That 'yeye' post dem put me no be am. Na outside cold I dey
since yesterday. Money to buy cigarette, sef, I no get. Sisi, I no
hold for hand.

Throws drink with head backward.

Dis one nain I for carry go yesterday. Dis 'Ogogoro' better pass
'oyinbo' own. He no dey give person headache. And you no go

feel one kind for morning. You go just dey kampe. Your body go just dey kakaraka.

Takes another drink. Barber clips and trims. Titi stares in admiration at soldiers gear and all.

NEWSPAPER MAN
(Prying from the corner of the newspaper)

My friend, I beg if no be say we get correct men fro this country, 'Oyinbo' don ban 'ogogoro' finish. Make we dey buy we own. And to buy our own, na prison. If to say Tai Solarin no halla dat time, 'oyinbo' factory go dey bring their own 'ogogoro', our own people no go work. And na our money dem go dey send go buy am from oversea. *('Se ti wa ni o mi o fe.. (BUY AFRIKA): Fela's music.)*

Puts newspaper a side, takes a shot. Soldier had sat down. Girl walk close to him, close up on grenade pin. Girl insert finger and pull it out. Soldier feeling the tug seeing the danger.

SOLDIER
Eewo, everybody down!

Remove grenade and throws it out.

SOLDIER
Everybody lie down! Take cover!

Slo-mo of bomb in the sky. Bounces off building wall. Everyone runs for cover. Bomb lands and roll on its axis. Sputtered and sputtered. Focus still on sputtering spark as it shuts out

18

Close Up on
Manufacture Date: October 1st 1969
Made In The Republic Of Biafra. "Buy Africa" play on "Viva
Nigeria"

SCENE 2, ACT 1

LONG SHOT INTERIOR

School Hallway / Passage DAY

It is a bright day. Students milling around with bags and books. Some with ipods in groups of 2,3 & 4. Jiving, talking and clenched first shakes. A student has a BLACK POWER Afrocomb stuck in the back of his head. TEACHER walks along hallway/ passage. He is dressed differently from students. More casual in African motif designs. Aged about 50, strong look, focused and futuristic.

AFRICA SHOULD STEM ITS BRAIN DRAIN AND PROMOTE THE AFRICAN RENAISSANCE. THE REBIRTH OF THE CONTINENT FOR AFRICA TO TAKE A CENTER STAGE IN TODAYS ECONOMIC WORLD, IT MUST GO OUT AND COMPETE ON A GLOBAL BASIS. - PHILLIP EMEGWALI

FOLLOW SHOT

Teacher gives BLACK POWER salute to a responding students, geared up in African symbolic greetings and all. Student gives clenched fist shake to colleague.

20

INTERIOR CLASS-DAY
FADE IN on class blackboard of the 5 music lines
ANGLE: Noisy as it can be. Teacher peeps through small door opening. Class unaware. Teacher shut door quietly.

INTERIOR SCHOOL HALLWAY / PASSAGE
Teacher checks watch while walking.

INTERIOR CLASS: *Minimum rowdiness. Time for class closes in Instrument boxes leaning against wall.*

FADE IN
Skin membrane of talking drum and jiggling bells in resounding process. The tightening hide emphasize rhythmic tonation. "RofoRofo fight" drumming of Tony Allen.

SHOT ON footwork/steps in harmony to talking drum. Dexerty is emphasized.

LONG SHOT Door opens. And Teacher comes in. Stands besides 3 Conga drums on stand as student hit away in succession at the Conga drum "JJD" (of Kofi). Appreciating the conga drummer who suddenly strikes the side gong in a multi rhythm calling the class to an attention ("Egbe! Wain!) SHOT goes to class stiffness. Attention and order.

Teacher walks to the middle of the class coughs the FELA cough.

TEACHER

Good morning, brothers and sisters, friends.

SHOT FADE IN ON students faces at the sudden already familiarity of the Teacher's greetings.

SHOT BACK ON TEACHER

I'll be teaching you ETHNOMUSICOLOGY. ETHNIC MUSIC 104 and I'll take you on CHOREOGRAPHY for 'jaara' as term project.
SHOT ON STUDENT with raised hand.

STUDENT

I am a Political Science major. I love music and I need to up my GPA. The choreography, I don't need. I can't even dance.

SHOT ON TEACHER

Choreography is an added value. This class is especially for you. Music is a universal language. The medium is the message. For political expressions, you need timing, space and theatrics to get your message across.

Our football team can't win matches. Because they can't dance. See Brazil, Cameron etc. they dance the samba and makossa on the play field.

Shot Back To Class As Students Look At Each Other Not Quite Grabbing The Message

TEACHER

There are three sources of power. One is violence, which is bestial, it requires no brain. Two, Wealth, which has gone out of fashion. The third is knowledge. You can't beat an intelligent man. Music is the weapon of the future. The man who don't read is worse than a man who can't read. I will teach you how to read music.

SHOT ON ANOTHER STUDENT

Music is mightier than the gun. Guitars, drums and the saxophone will replace all the AK 47, tanks and bombs.
SHOT from Teacher's Angle

TEACHER

You are right. And for the purpose of this class, we shall study the works of the greatest African that ever lived. His visions and aspiration of a renascent Africa is the central theme of his repertoire. He was a maestro. A master. A musicologist. He was the greatest thing to come at of Africa since Kwame Nkrumah.

Brothers, sisters, friends, we shall understudy and research FELA ANIKULAPO-KUTI, and his disdain and disenchantment for African elites.

His music is ritual theatre. Its is not dance hall music. The music of Fela is ideological, Political with a singular theme, AFRICANISM. To understand his music, you must share his political philosophy. Felasophy!

FADE ON FELA ANKULAPO-KUTI

The African Personality of an Enigma
The Primary man of an African Personality.

SCENE 2, ACT 2

DAY IN A CLASS

1ST STUDENT

Christopher Okigbo literature is futuristic. He must be with the angels now.

2ND STUDENT

But he failed to see the extent of the damage ahead. The country should have gone beyond Aburi.

1ST STUDENT

This nation has failed Africa. Chris was in the war for peace. He felt for his kith and kin. There shouldn't have been an Ahiara Declaration

3RD STUDENT

How come they keep taking from Africa? Now they are taking Fela's music. Took our religion. Gave us their own. They enforced their language and debased our language and ways of life.

2ND STUDENT

The genocide in Sudan is crime against humanity. It's an ongoing systematic campaign.
Omar Bashir is using Arab 'janjanweed' militias to murder and rape black Sudanese. The Chinese are financing the genocide.

3RD STUDENT

This is a crime of intention. Bashir wants to exterminate Fur, Masalit and Zaghawa people in Sudan for its oil This is where 20 men rape one woman, creating 'janjanweed' babies, an explosion of infanticide.

VARIETIES IS THE SPICE OF LIFE, OTHER CULTURES AND CIVILIZATION MUST BE ALLOWED TO THRIVE ALONG SIDE THOSE OF THE WEST. AND MORE IMPORTANTLY, THERE HAS TO BE AN END TO THE EXORCIST MENTALITY OF THE WEST.

Wole Soyinka

SCENE 3, ACT 1

EXTERIOR SHOT ON Kalakuta Republic smoking, hair pleating, swimming, loafing and music instrument practice. SHOT ON Fela in the living room in under wear. His saxophone on stand in a corner. Girl sit on armchair rest make up and all. wall mural of afrika 70 man stand with rolled poster trying to catch trying Fela's attention.

MAN

Fela, some person just come say dem want make you come lecture dem for ideology *(spreads poster for Fela's attention.)*

YOUNG AFRICAN PIONEERS
University of Ibadan

PRESENTS

AFRIKAN CONSCIOUSNESS &EMANCIPATION
The thoughts of KWAME NKRUMAH

Venue: TRENCHARD HALL
Time: 3:00pm
WAKE UP! IT IS TIME FOR CONSCIENSCISM

AFRIKA WILL UNITE!

FELA
Where dem dey?

MAN
Dem dey outside

FELA
Let dem come in

Shot on door opening
Remi, Fela's wife comes in

FELA
Eh! Remi How are you?

REMI
I'm fine. How have you been?

FELA
I dey. How are the children?

REMI
They are doing well. They all miss you. Fela, I need to talk to you. In private.

FELA
Give me a minute. Please sit down (patting a sit beside him)

REMI
I can't stay long. Yeni is babysitting, You know she is still a little girl, too.

SHOT / FOCUS ON Fela as he gets up goes to balcony.
Focus on Fela and Remi camera from inner living room focus as well.

27

REMI

I have got this new place. I have to raise the children away from Kalakuta. And my health, I need a quiet place.

FELA

Are you sure you'll be alright there? If you need to get a bigger place, please do. I will make available the money including furnishing and you'll need a car, tabi?

REMI

What we have, will do. I don't want to come too hard on you. You know I love you as those other girls do. I understand your position. No hard feelings *(goes over and hugged and kissed Fela the two embrace .... For a moment)*.

REMI

The children ask when you are coming to cook those African food.

FELA

(Fela laughed) You know it is my house, too, I fit come anytime.

SHOT ON Remi as she walks away through the living room. Fela walks from balcony through living room to his seat.

SCENCE 4, ACT 1

Camera shot on round table. National Association of Poets, Writers and Artistes (NAPWA) it is a round table discussion session. A sort of workshop

RAWSHID

I am not an establishment man but I have dined and wined with them. What they do is quiet different from what they tell the people. I kind of feel bad when I am categorized as one of them.

Though I earn my living working with them. But I do not work for them to promote their nefarious activities.

Gentlemen, there are these gargantuan projects which the people believe it is meant for their own interest, the so-called project are designed to steal from people and share the loot.

The World Bank knows it. The developed world knows this. They turn their back to these....

OSAHON

Long shot on round table

Rasheed, just let me come in. The whiteman, Brentwood, Paris Club, World Bank. IMF never like us black people. I know them. The only thing they admire in us is the BLACK POWER. Their woman like our big penis. The men like our artistic phenomenon. Our athletic prowess and sportsmanship. They have stolen so much from us, they don't do much for us. They don't seem to want to stop.

Right now, we have to create an awareness in all our fronts. All hands must be on deck. All boot must be on the ground for the future of Africa.

Palmwine is served in calabash cups

FELA

Brothers, we have to start right here to have that consciousness. We have to free our people from these Eurocentric attitude. You see, I had to withdraw my children from school when soldiers, soldiers! were running our schools. Now they have been let loose on our streets. You see soldiers and police beating and flogging up pedestrians, traffic offenders and traders on the street. Even to the face of their wives and children. It is African culture to sell at the road side. These supermarket shopping is European. Solders should stay in their 'bareke'. There should be a check on all these uniformed men harassing people. What's so spectacular about the uniform? Sebi , uniform na cloth, na tailor dey sew am.

WS

I have been abused, jailed, chased out of my country by power drunken soldiers in government. I will not compromise my stand against power abuse and oppression.

What this country is going through is a shame. What we have are mediocres and desktop generals. We shall continue to fight them with all the resources available to us. Their promises to hand over to elected government lack any sincerity of purpose. And if, and when they do, it is going to be a recycling of military apologists and their dummies.

PROFESSOR

As long as we do not have a base as a country. We are not a nation in the real sense of it. Our indigenous bases of authority has been eroded. They are all now replaced by retired establishment men who were part of the problems then.

Look at our political culture. The cultural foundations, politics and religious structure of the indigenous African societies have been dismantle and upturned by European colonialism.

As 'Go slow' play .. " man must be man for his land:.."

Focus on Fela

FELA

That is why you see African with English names. As for me, I have change my name to FELA ANIKUKLAPO KUTI. That one has a meaning. The meaning of RANSOME I know. The white man cannot hold me to ransome again. You see, the African Personality and mentality must be restored. We must regain our self confidence, self-reliance and our capacity for independence as a man must be replaced.

We cannot continue to follow-follow, and mimic them. Our leaders are blind. They are chosen because they have low mentality. They know the ones with colo-mentality who can't think beyond material things. According to all the wealth in Africa we should not be the poorest. They think they are keeping us down. They are down with us, too.

RAWSHID

The word economy is supply and demand. Africa is a buyers market. There is no way we can be a supply economy if we keep buying from them. We have been a dumping market for all kinds of garbage from their factories. My brothers, with the multinationals here, we are in deep shit.

FELA

The multinationals, they use slave labour to produce obsolete products different from the ones produced in America and Europe. And Africans are directors, and chairmen. Everyday, they fill out hundreds of FORM A and Forum M to transfer millions to their home countries, under several false over invoicing and fake import applications. You think they are going to take it easy? Our people should buy AFRICAN products, Made in AFRICA, We must embrace African industries, services and attitudes. The corruption of our mind must stop.

Shots of Fela chewing stick and several slots of his costumes

As for me, I do not use the tooth paste. I use the chewing stick. I bath with the black soap from natural ingredients. No caustic soda. I use the shea butter for my hair and coconut oil for the skin. If I want a baby soft skin, I use the camwood to enhance the tenderness. We should patronize the neighborhood shoemaker, and tailors.

Your money goes to Saville Row and Seventh Avenue. Your brother here will make a correct attire that will free your mind from colomentality.

BUY AFRIKA. BUY MADE IN AFRIKA

Camera Focus on

Palmwine is served, Ogogoro is served Akara, Jogi, Alapa, wara, aadun. etc.

KWAME

Close up shot

This is a country where culture means corruption, Ethics means bribery. Intergrity means stealing, this country is a mess. Here's a country where nothing works and nobody talks. No electricity, no running water, no sense of belonging, no jobs.

SCENE 5, ACT 1

Man comes in startle
Fela! Fela! Fela! Police don come.

FELA

Again? Say wetin happen?

MAN

Dem dom enter Kalakuta. Dem just de molest everybody.

FELA

Dem enter? (*A stampede of all manners crashed into the living room followed by gun shots outside.*)
SHOT EXT FOCUS On Police / Soldiers assaulting in a most abusive manner.

SHOT BACK IN LIVING ROOM INTERIOR
Fela rush into room bring out a bag. Orders everyone to start eating contents

SCENE 6, ACT I

FELA

Oya, make una dey chop.

Focus on gulping and munching away handful of contents.

Door burst open. Cops soldiers astonished as entire household is eating away evidence and the purpose of crashing into Fela's household.

Shot on cop soldiers looking at each other in shock.

FELA

What do you want here?

INSPECTOR

We have a warrant for your arrest.

FELA

Wetin I do?

INSPECTION

Abduction of teenage girls and possession of and use of Indian Hemp.

FELA

SHOT BACK TO FELA STILL CHEWING'

You see am for my hand?

INSPECTOR

But we have orders for your arrest. Please come with us to the station.

SCENE 7, ACT 1

ALAGBON CLOSE
In police station. Fela sits behind counter. Angle shots from yonder cells. Shot of cell and sorry suspects.

The entry board has Fela's name against possession, abduction of teenage girls.
The arresting Inspector comes in and looks Fela over. Goes into charge room.
Stands at attention before AC.

AREA COMMANDER
Inspector, what do we have?

INSPECTOR
The suspect has been brought in, sir.

AREA COMMANDER
Do you have anything against him?

INSPECTOR
He chop the exhibit

AREA COMMANDER
Chop wetin? That man!

INSPECTOR
But we can still nail him. The girls are young. Underage.

AREA COMMANDER
Were they under lock and key? It is not a commune of any sort?

INSPECTOR
Sir, you should see the criminality of the whole place. They were just smoking Igbo like no man's business.

AREA COMMANDER
Any exhibit?

SCENE 8, ACT 1

Fela in cell with other suspects. 1st inmate is an accountant, Fraud suspect. Officer check roll

1ST INMATE
Fela sing for us now *(Fela sings. Another officer brings new suspect.)*

2ND INMATE
What do you have for us?

NEW INMATE
Nothing. They took all my money and the pack of cigarette.

2ND INMATE
What's your charge?

NEW INMATE
Wandering. Said I was walking without a genuine reason. And I don't understand it. Is it in statutory code?
(Voice from cell interior)
Giam one!

New inmate receives slap from nowhere
And falls over. Opening his eyes, he was at camera level staring into the face of FELA. But blinkingly.

NEW INMATE
What is my offence again?
Voice (from cell interior) Oya, stand up, FUCK ALHAJA!

*As he struggles to get up. A hand pulls him up drags him to the
wall.*
Above his head is window (2x2) with iron rods
Voice (from cell interior)
Oya FUCK ALHAJA!
Teach him how to do it.
*New inmate is seen hanging with finger tips. Feet off the ground.
Pelvic moves in the manner of fucking.*
Cell opens. Officer calls out.
ORDER!

SCENE 9, ACT 1

OFFICER

Fela, a visitor for you.

Fela is seen sitting across a table facing Mom.
Mom is backing camera "Omo Iya Aje" yell from cell.

MOM

They said you ate it. And they are taking your shit for forensic analysis. So, here is bitter leaf with ogiri. I have some amala. If you want.

FELA

Beere. The vegetable will do.

MOM

Sweetness is the essence of the bitter leaf.
If leaves sweet taste in the end.

SCENE 10, ACT 1

INSPECTOR
We will nail him. Send his shit to Oshodi for analysis.

AREA COMMANDER (Smiling)
That's something. Inspector, honestly, I don't have anything against this man. He is just bohemian. The message of his music is causing some discomfort in some quarters. Not here, I believe.

INSPECTOR
Fela is a dangerous musician and he is creating a consciousness, an awareness with his music. His music is subversive.

AREA COMMANDER
Don't you think his objectives will do us all a lot of good. Moreover, the music is fantastic.

INSPECTOR
What do I do with him, sir,

AREA COMMANDER
Book him! Throw the bugger in cell.

INSPECTOR
Alright sir, *(turns to go. As he reaches door.)*

AREA COMMANDER
I hope you can stand the heat that comes after this. *Door shots.*

41

SCENE 11, ACT 1

EXTERIOR COURT PROMISES

SHOT ON FELA carried shoulder high on body guard's shoulder.
Fela longshot in clenched BLACK POWER fist salute. Crowd milling around in jubilation. Forensic analysis NEGATIVE Expensive Shit music of FELA playing
CLOSE up on REPORTER with microphone. Others with mike and cable extends to tape recorder on the side

1ST REPORTER

Fela, How do you feel at your acquittal?

FELA

What do you think? The judge has more sense that the police. The police who will jail me, dem never born am.

1ST REPORTER

You have just got off a possible ten year jail term for possession. Isn't that remarkable for all the evidence against you.

FELA

Possession of what? Indian Hemp. I've never been to Indian. They took my shit for analysis. The result was negative. That prosecutor claim say I chop am. He took my shit brought in as exhibit. Isn't that remarkable? My shit is exhibit. They still have it. They may want to appeal. It must not lost.

Legalized it sort of but regulated and controlled. Half of the world does it. I smoke NNG. Nigeria Natural Grass from

Obiaruku. It does not contain tetrahydrocarabinol (TTC) In Nigeria, corruption, authority stealing is legalized. So legalize NNG!

Focus on 2nd Reporter

2ND REPORTER

This is an abuse on your fundamental human right, in your own house. And what you do to your body without endangering anyone is your business. Are you going to file a suit for infringement on your right and forcibly breaking and entry into your premises.

FELA

Suit ke? No, it is a finished matter. But dem go hear pansapansa.
Focus TV Reporter

TV REPORTER

Close up shot
This is the court premises of the magistrate court. Fela has been acquitted from the misdemeanor charges brought against him for possession of cannabis sativa. He will not file a counter suit. Instead, Fela will resume his performances at the African Shrine to night. This is WNTV Obotunde Ijimere reporting
Focus on Kanmi Isola Osobu

OSOBU

(Quoting John Stuart Mill)
The individual is sovereign over himself, over his own body and mind. What Fela does to himself is his business.

SCENE 12, ACT 1

It is early morning hour about 5 am Christian / Muslim prayer call in the background. Crowd come out of shrine entrance. Youngster seen having drinks. One offers cigarette to another. Rejects offer. Another offer a joint to same youngster. Again he rejects offer. All three walk away. Motorcycle sounds roars. Lamplight on camera.

Stop with headlamps beams on screen. Cut engine. Lamps out. Camera focus on rider's high knee boot.

Youngster walks toward Rider and bike. He is a police on patrol, Sgt. Tefe.

SERGENT

Una go Fela Shrine go smoke marijuana, abi? O ya, make I search una, *(He moves close to the 'cool' youngster Thrust this hand in his side pocket. Camera focus on joint between fingers. Hand goes into the boy's side pocket without anyone seeing the deception. On emerging, Sergent Tefe's hand comes up with the 'joint' holding it up for everyone to see.*

SERGENT

Shot on Cop

I don't catch you. Una dey smoke Igbo, abi?

To the boys bewilderment, between protest and I beg sir', 'please, sir'

SERGENT

Close up shot

Oya, make we go 'tation. I beg no dey for this one. Una know say na 10 years for prison.

44

1ST YOUNGSTER

Long shot of all
Officer, Dis one no dey smoke. His father is a Reverend

SERGENT

Focus on Cop
Him Papa na Reverend. Then, Fela Papa nko, no be Reverend?
So, na my Papa be winch? na devil born me. O ya make we go
station

2ND YOUNGSTER

You can't take him and leave us. You will have to take the three of
us. *(The youngsters not understanding the situation).*

SERGENT

Shot on coyly cop
O ya, wetin una wan do? Naim be say, the three of una go go
prison

CULPRIT YOUNGSTER

Still astonished
Officer, I don't smoke. But how come it got in my pocket?

SERGENT

Shot on all
So you are calling me a liar? You wan teach me my job? *(moves
and hold boy at trousers waistband. Pulls him closer)*

2ND YOUNGSTER

Officer, this is not right.

CULPRIT YOUNGSTER

I will submit myself to blood analysis. I will prove this is wrong.

SERGENT

But I found this is your possession. It will be your words against mine. Ole! Una fit be armed robbers sef.

CULPRIT YOUNGSTER

Close up shot on
Officer na wa for you o! How can you do this to people? Do I look like a thief?

SERGENT

Shot on
After all I didn't say I caught you stealing. It is just a misderneanour charge. Possession. And you know what the penalty is. 10 years with hard labour.

1ST YOUNGSTER

Camera close on
Awaiting Inspector! *(Sergent smiles at the futuristic promotional address)* what do you want us to do now we don't want to go to the station Moreover, your motorcycle can only take just one person.

SERGENT

Who tell you? If u na be ten, I go carry all of una reach Station.

2ND YOUNGSTER

Officer, this one you arrested doesn't smoke. It is us two that smoke. How you got that thing from his pocket is magic.

SERGENT

So, you mean say, I commot rabbit from inside like Professor Peller.

CULPRIT YOUNGSTER

Close up

No! No! you are not a magician. You did not even say "abracadabra" before the "Igbo" emerged. Look officer, we know what's up. What do you want from us?

SERGENT

Close up shot

So una sabi? Why una come dey do like say una no know wetin dey happen?

A group of mean looking men walk by smoking the 'funny cigarette'

MAN

Awari Tefe! You don catch one. Abi na three?

2ND MAN

Money don plenty

3RD MAN

Tefe, the Goldfinger. Boys make una settle am. Man must wack now.

Group walk on. Not waiting. After a few meters from "scene of crime"

3RD MAN

Shot on

He used to be a pickpocket at the bus stop. His last trick was right inside the bus. They almost lynched him. Then he joined the police

SCENE 13, ACT 1

DAY
Interior. University campus Auditorium. Students are seated. On the rostrum is a speaker. clad in black t-shirt, and jeans. And a black beret.
Bearded or not, it doesn't matter.
A banner hangs behind the high table and another at the back of the auditorium titles:

(1)   AFRICA IS OUR FUTURE.
(2)   AFRICA OF TOMORROW
(3)   AFRICAN CONSCIOUSNESS

Sire, nurture, protect and give succour to africanism: the ultimate reality.

KWAME OGUN
One of the most dangerous thing in the world is to steal from your people. The African elites were stealing from the poor. And when your steal from the poor, you're gambling with your life.

TOURE SANKORE
The war against corruption will just have to be restructured because government is inept. They use the pen to rob the treasury.

KWAME OGUN
African intellectuals in dispora must come back for a renascent Africa.

SCENE 14, ACT 1
DAY DEFENCE HQ
Shot on officer at his desk. Colonel is sitting opposite

COMMANDING OFFICER
We can't go in the Shrine. We will attract the higher-ups to this miscreant?

COLONEL
He has this newest composition. It is pungent, irritating and a disrespect to the army. It is worse. Na Zombie.

COMMANDING OFFICER
ZOMBIE! Do you know what you are saying. ZOMBIE is a macabre dead. Unreasoning. Takes orders. You mean the CIC and the IG sit in that marijuana den and enjoy the bullshit this punk is spitting at us. Who else come in there?

COLONEL
Naval Capt. Wole Bucknor. They were together with Victor Olaiya and S.O'. s son the one at NIDB.

COMMANDER OFFICER
Get ready to storm Kalakuta. We will use the storm troopers from Abalti. This time we shall kill the motherfucker. What about that officers daughter?

COLONEL
She ran back to Kalakuta

COMMANDER OFFICER
What does he do to them? Juju them?

COLONEL
No sir, Fela has a charming personality. The girls just love the bulge between his legs. They see him as a sex symbol.

COMMANDING OFFICER
I am going to break his balls and then bayonet the prick. ZONE B OR ZOMBIE we will surely smell his own shit this time.

COLONEL
Yes, sir!

COMMANDING OFFICER
Dismiss!

SCENE 15, ACT 1

Camera on Fela. As S.M. speaks off camera.

SERGENT MAJOR

Where were you at the civil war? Can't even fight for the unity of a country you keep mouthing about?

FELA

You call this a country? This is not even a nation. It is a CUNT- ry. As in pussy. Toto!

Fighting, shooting, killings, especially children and women. Is that the path to peace? And unity.

SERGEANT MAJOR

How come you indict a system that sent the sons of us working class to fight wars. The majority of you, the sons of the middle and upper class avoid it.

FELA

Those wars could have been avoided. To have peace we don't have to kill and destroy. War is an extension of politics.

SERGEANT MAJOR

I have been there. You never was.

FELA

I am in music. The weapon of the future. Not guns and bombs.

SERGEANT MAJOR

You might as well tell me the pen is in mightier than the gun.

SCENE 16, ACT 2

DAY IN FELA'S LIVING ROOM
Fela and Rawshid in a tete a-tete.

FELA

You are an economist. What does economy mean? I know it is not supply and demand as you defined it.

RAWSHID

Economics is the production of goods and services paid for by the consumer.

FELA

Is it not he-con-me? Or is it 'e kan no mi' in Yoruba meaning 'they garb it up once' which means fraud and corruption.

RAWSHID

No. it can't mean that. But it is in the obvious literary meaning. You could say it meant so. In an advance economy. It is not so.

FELA

It is more so in an advance economy where the poor people are oppressed by the few rich.

RAWSHID

Coming from an elite family, I understand your feel for these wretched of the earth. But we were all part of the problem.

FELA

I am an Africanist. Africanism is ancient. Deep rooted in the traditional African society. It is respectable. Very heavy in culture.

RAWSHID

Fela, will it bring utopia? The perfect state?

FELA

Close up

No. No. Don't get me wrong. I despise utopia. It is catastrophic. It is bad for creativity and humanity. You see, pan Africanism began with liberation struggle of Afican- Americans expressing aspiration of Africa and people of African descent.
Sylvester Williams, W.E.B DuBois, Marcus Garvey and George Padmore were not born in Africa. Yet they wanted an Africa free from the West. Kwame Nkrumah rekindle the concept of the African Personality.

RAWSHID

Shot on

Nkrumah was a most misunderstood man. Azikiwe had a dose of being mis-understood, too. The Europeans and American would not want an emerging African. A renascent Africa will be a threat to their socio-political economy. It will give black people all over the world a sense of belonging and self-assurance that their homeland has become a force to be reckoned with in the world geo-politics.

FELA

Close up

I don't know why African rulers, dem no be leaders, allow themselves to be used to disrupt their people and suck their treasury dry. They don't think at all and can't read between the lines. They don't know a traitor is not needed when the treason is complete. <u>Look at Mobutu.</u> Can you imagine how he could slaughter Lumumba on CIA orders. Killing his own brother. See MKO, he drank tea. See Obasanjo, he is running out of time. He don sink. He never know. The CIA are finally going to get his ass. He is their boy. Like MKO.

RAWSHID

Close up shot

Fela, look CIA killed JFK- one of their own. Why? Because he was getting too people oriented. And they don't like such extremism.

SCENE 17, ACT 1

DAY. LOCATION SHOT
Interior university campus lecture wall poster reads: AFRIKA WILL UNITE: Young African Pioneers

FELA

On stage addressing
The press with dia yeye foto; the so called media treat me as a degenerate and corrupter of youth. They say I demonize the youth.

Fela move about on stage
What they have failed to understand is the ideology of my music. Afrobeat is erotic theatre, intelligent and sensitive. It is not dance hall music. My music is a political statement.
After I read about great black men, my eyes opened to the essence of my Africaness.

My music took a different turn. I play the music of Africa. I sing about blackism and the emancipation of my people from oppressive rules and foreign control. As if Africa is a piece of cake, they carve it into pieces at the Berlin Conference of 1884.

FELA
DAY IN THE CAFETERIA
Fela standing on table

56

What was left from slavery became formally owned. This period of colonization saw Africa in its worst condition. Even though colonization gave way to nationalism. It looks like liberation but it could not restore the ideal traditional African society. It became an indirect subjection to the dictates of Europe. Our independence was an alienation from African traditional society; a raisin in the sun! Our value system was misplaced.

(Fela walking around in crowded hall)
We took on the whiteman's ways of life putting our own down as primitive and vernacular. We must emerge from this obscurity and *(Fela sitting among students crowding around him).* Come into the open to earn our greatness. Because we wanted to be civilized, we ceased to be African. To embrace this new standard, Britain committedly imposed their imperials on us. You have to talk big grammar, dress like them, speak through the nose, eat their food using fork and knife, embracing all their culture and tradition. As for the French, it was "assimilation". Others used Christian beatitude to disorient the African. While they stole our land and pride, we were clutching the bible looking up to the heavens asking for miracles and salvations.(Church service in session)

SCENE 18, ACT 1

LOCATION SHOT: DEFENCE HQ ZOOM INTO WINDOW. AS VOICE OVER OF C. O.

COMMANDING OFFICER

All is set for attack. First, cut off the electricity supply. Twenty minutes later, blow up the generator. Cut the barb wire fence. Then smoke them all out. Tear gas the building. Sight target. Draw him out. I want 20 men on him. Beat him to a pulp. Then, I will personally bayonet the blighter. He is getting too big for his mouth.

SHOT BACK TO LECTURE HALL

FELA

Nationalism in Africa is subversion that requires police beatings. African governments were getting technical aid to Africa which was designed to keep us undeveloped. We have failed to recognize and appreciate the models of early African society which had a merchant economy. Their own economic model structures have failed us. They have to continually come to our aid in every which way they can. We had an African Iron Age using metal technology in 400 B.C, before dem born Jesus Christ. Our farming was advanced after the 7th millennium before Christianity. Africa gave rice to the world. Before Independence, African societies disintegration was appalling. There was

58

breakdown of traditional African custom. Agriculture deteoriated.

Shot on Fela in a village square atmosphere.
The model system in the villages collapsed and there was massive exodus to the cities.
Worst still, Government concentrated development to the urban cities leaving the rural areas to rot. The villages were underdevelopment with an ever exploding urban population.
So, what we have was overpopulation, under-production of food, mal-distribution of goods and services.

Fela on soap box in the street corner.
This is the legacy of colonialism inherited by our nationalist. Europe saw this as a continuity of slavery. That is why you see our women, use mercury bleaching for their skin, perming their hair, their toto hair nko? Dey should perm that, too. Na that time I go open shop. Shenshenma! *(Music of Shenshenma).*

Fela: In his house
Even our football is governed by decree. FIFA just dey look as we dey destroy ourselves. African leaders inherited their dictatorial style. With bureaucracy, there is nepotism. Paddy-Paddy government is the goldmine for wealth. You see them sharing splitting contract and over-invoicing. They just steal and share money. That is the inheritance of colomentality. After the World War 2, Britain and France

squeezed and exploited Africa like never before. Go and read Walter Rodneys. 'How Europe Underdeveloped Africa' Dr. Ben Joachana- "Blackman of the Nile". What they have done was to destroy and downgrade African institution and culture which, through our long history had taught us how to provide checks and balance, public control over executive excesses and distrust.

Camera shots on Empires of Africa ,Oyo ,Benni, Ghana, Bornu, Mali and Songhai.
Empires of a past Africa had a developed form of government. There pre-colonial forms involves public participation. This could have been a useful concept for an evolved postcolonial form of government.
Their political science don't teach African history because they are ignorant of our past. Go and study the governments of the old Oyo Empire, Benin Empire, Ghana Empire, Mali, Songhai, Kanem Bornu. Those were great times, brothers and sisters.

Shots of star studded heavens
The first University in the world, was in Timbuktu. The Dogon tribe of Mali know more of the celestial stars than any astrologer with their big telescopes. NASA go to them for tutorials. We taught the European everything he knows. What we did not teach him, he stole. We had well designed cities in Benin, the whiteman was astonished at our level of development. See what they did to Ovaremen Nogbaisi.

Look, we have to start kicking asses, too. Enough is enough.
Close up on Fela in sitting room full of guest
We should stop sending cocoa to them. We will process it to
Eruku Oshodi, sell it to them. If dem like make dem no buy
am. Our cocoa farmers no dey kuku chop chocolate. Na
dem chocolate dey hungry. Who tell you say we no get
technology. We invented the wheel. Now do you think we
built the pyramid. Abi, Egypt no be Africa?

Shot on
Fela and His Egypt 80 band

SCENE 19, ACT 1

Court Premises: Ambulance is parked outside

SHOT OF COURT INTERIOR.
JUDGE

I understand the defendant is not in court.

OSOBU

Close up shot
He is in the court premises. My client is not in good health, My Lord

JUDGE

Then where's he?

OSOBU

He is in the ambulace *Outside. There is an emergency.* He is on the way to surgery in another 10 minutes, My Lord.

JUDGE

Camera shot on Judge
Can I see the Doctor's report and recommendation.

OSOBU

Here, My Lord
Osobu give it to the court clerk.

JUDGE

Close up looking from above rim

The court shall proceed to sight the defendant on his sick bed.

Court rise to exit courtroom towards ambulance. Hospital Assistant opens door. Fela is lying on stretcher. surrounded by retinue of girls and P. A's Judges peers in above the rim of eye glass. Judge mumbles sympathy turns back.

JUDGE

Close up in court

The case cannot proceed. To save the court time; I dismiss this abduction case against the defendant. *(Hammers gravel)*

COURT!

SCENE 20, ACT 1

Interior Fela's livingroom. The press, crowd around FELA

FELA

The greatest problem facing Africa today is Colo-Mentality, which has given birth to second slavery. We have to do away with Eurocentric and America influence. Africa's greatness depends on political unity. No African country can develop in isolation. The effect of isolation has been vicious. What we have on ground now is poverty, corruption, oppression and injustice. We need political integration to plan for economic development which will enhance social growth and the African Personality. A continental socio-political economy will bring back Africa to the comity of nations. This 1884 Berlin Conference partition is divisive and oppressive. Go and see the blueprint of the Economic Commission for Africa of 1958 by Kwame Nkrumah.

We should nurture our culture and history to develop that African Personality for an educational and intellectual foundation for Africa. The forces that unite us will be greater than our differences. Then the goal to establish an African dignity, progress and prosperity will be achieved.

SHOT ON PRESS

1ST PRESS

Fela, why did you not participate in the FESTAC '77 colloquim, to present your `aspiration?

FELA

The Obasanjo government is the perfect prostitution of a military government. Military government shamelessly fell on Africa in their imperialist adventure to ensure the continue hold on Africa by Europe and America. Their objective is to halt and disrupt the growth of Africa.

The objectives of FESTAC 77 was to ensure the revival, resurgence, propagation and promotion of black and African cultural values and civilization. A return to the origin.

At the shrine

FELA

Festac was to bring to light the diverse contributions of black and African people to the universal currents of thoughts and arts, by facilitating our acceptance and access to a better international and inter-racial understanding.

SCENE 21, ACT 1

DAWN. *Fela's Shrine. Show just ended. Sit in relaxed mood.*

FELA

I have always been dedicated to the attainment of total African freedom. Total emancipation of Africa especially from second slavery, we must have political union of African states to safeguard our independence and the foundation for our individual, economic, social and cultural advancement. In one word, freedom and unification of Africa. (looks to Stevie Wonder, who nods in agreement)

Close up shot
This government just wasted money on FESTAC. To them it was another jamboree to steal.
The primary objective was a unified policy and action for progress and development to shut away foreign hold, aids and recommendations.

We can only meet them effectively with a united front and continental purpose.

As long as a single country in Africa is governed by puppet governments manipulated form Europe and America, Africa is open to danger and underdevelopment.

The African Personality will resist sinister threat and designs of the west in our political union.

2ND PRESS
You sound like a racist in your aspiration for Africa.

Shot on Fela

FELA
I am not a racist
Slavery was not born out of racism. Racism was the consequence of slavery. Racism brought out the myth of colour inferiority. Don't let us paint the truth. Europeans who sought, set sail to seize African states, were thinking of for themselves, working for their own profit and conquering for spoils of war and power. The origin of colonization is an economic enterprise of European interest. A one sided egoistical imposition. Colonization is not an act of civilization or formulated to civilize. It is an act of force motivated by interest.

The greatness of Africa depends on political unity. Says Kwame Nkrumah
SEEK FIRST THE POLITICAL FREEDOM. EVERYTHING WILL FOLLOW KWAME NKRUMAH

3RD PRESS
What does Africa have to offer the world today?

Close up shot

FELA
Intelligence.
Touching his head with index finger

SCENE 22 ACT I

BEKO/FELA'S BULLET PROOF JUJU

In Fela's living room in Kalakuta- sober atmosphere

BEKO

I understand your need for protection against this military government assault especially, the shootings.

FELA

They cant' kill me, I have got the power. This is African bullet proof. Their machine gun can't even touch me.
Pulls at Amulet/hanging on neck

BEKO

You have to be really careful. We all love you. We don't want to lose you so soon

FELA

Dem no fit. Dem no born dem well.

BEKO

Have you really tested this thing?

FELA

Beko, I know you don't believe in anything. You have a scientific mind. To you, anything unscientific is not true. You don't even believe in the Supreme being.

BEKO

Fela, my belief has nothing to do with that thing hanging on your neck.

Don't argue with a man with a gun.

FELA

(Pulls at other amulet) This is owo. It is heavy.

BEKO

Without this one, you still command a high regard of yourself. It is your personality. You have a charming personality. You don't need that charm to have it.

FELA

Beko, I beg, let's stop this argument

BEKO

Okay I agree. But let's test these amulets. *(Shot at goat, hanging from its necks are Fela's charms.) Beko aims. Pulls trigger. Fela's astonished as goats falls dead. Amulets ineffective!*

SCENE 23, ACT I

Day. Fela's House

Fela Chewing stick
Stick-down up, teeth, tongue and gums in grunts and throat cleanings.

FELA

Fluoride has been banned all over the world for use in tooth paste and drinking water. But in Africa, where we have the strongest teeth according to WHO, our government still allow the use of fluoride. Fluoride is bad for the teeth. But the importer and supplier of fluoride is a big man. A stupid man. Destroying his own people so he can make money.

SCENE 24, ACT I

KALAKUTA SHOW

SHOT on a man on ladder. He is disconnecting a main power line. Another shot on a police officer on horse back. Reflecting sun glasses reflects the neighborhood as he passes by on patrol.

SCENE 24, ACT II

Fela's Kalakuta Republic is in back ground. Band boys and residents mingle around. The swimming pool is crowded. SHOT BACK ON MAN on ladder rungs. As he disconnects. Power outage spread. Curse and cursings on NEPA.

SCENE 24, ACT III

Shots on reactions
SHOT BACK to kalakuta Republic's generator as it roars to life.

SCENE 24, ACT IV

SHOT ON ceiling fan coming to full revolution speed. Fela is seen in his underwear with guest all over the living room. A press conference of a sort is in progress. Steve Wonder dey there, too. Owning up to his Africaness. Corn row braids and sunglasses.

SCENE 24, ACT V

Long shot of sitting room as door burst open.

YOUNGSTER

Fela! Dem don come again, Police, Soldier.

FELA

Say wetin happen again?

Fela goes to balcony sees the confusion on the ground below. The barbed wire is being cut Soldiers have surrounded the compound. The girls are manhandled, sex handled, rough handled. The boys are running all over the place. The generator is shot at, bursting unto flames. Guests in Fela's livingroom are seen hurdled outside to safety. Fela joins in the melee.

FELA

What's the meaning of all this? You can't just come to people house and start kicking everybody around. What's all this shit about?

SHOT ON officer with rifle / bayonet sights Fela. Closes up on him in the middle of the cacophony as he gets to Fela. He raises the rifle's butt and knocks Fela down. Fela goes down. Blood from broken skull and kicking him ..... Back to the house. Now on fire. Smoke envelopes the neighborhood. Crowd gathers. An army cordones off the area.

SHOT BACK on Fela staring at a raised bayonet from Fela eye view.

OFFICER (With bayonet)
Die! You over-political bastard!

Shot on Fela's guitarist Ogene Kologbo dives to cover Fela from bayonet. He gets the stab. And manages to pick Fela up to safety. Teargas, shots. Explosions. Pandemoium. Beatings, Writhing pain etc.

Camera closes on as Fela's Mom, is hurled through window.

SHOT ON SCREEN
An inquiry was commissioned to give a situation report on the Kalakuta show. The Justice Agu Anya Tribunal submitted that an "Unknown soldier" set Fela's house on fire including other houses in the neighborhood. The affected land were confisicated and acquired by the Federal Military Government of Nigeria. Fela and other 2,000 citizens were rendered homeless. No alternative accommodation was provided. The tribunal reinstated that Fela cannot have a Republic within the Republic of Nigeria. Therefore, there cannot be a Kalakuta Republic within the territorial integrity of Nigeria.

SCENE 25, ACT 1

LONG SHOT ON DEFENCE HQ, LAGOS

Close upon officers orderly as they proceed along hallway. Orderly opens door to let officer in at attention others respond.
Sitted on desk. Others sitting too.

COMMANDING OFFICER

Shall we have the security report

COLONEL

The report we have here is contradictory. Though the possession case has been dismissed. The abduction of the teenage girls case is still pending. We want to appeal.

COMMANDING OFFICER

Then what do we have?

COLONEL

Security reports says he is still militant. Especially his barbs and jibes at the military.
And sir, several of our officers are regulars at the shrine too.

COMMANDING OFFICER

How high?

COLONEL

The C.I.C frequents the place. And they seem very close. The IG is his close friend.

COMMANDING OFFICER
Does it mean we can't bring the place down. The CIC just cut down penalty for possession to 6 months or N200 fine.

COLONEL
Yes sir, he does not own the place .The owner will be glad to have us kick him out. He is becoming too much from him. I gathered he has not been paying his rents lately.

COMMANDING OFFICER
Who owns the place?

COLONEL
Empire Kanu.

C.O
Do you have the tribunal report?

COLONEL
Yes, sir. And it says he can't have a republic within the Republic of Nigeria. That is, his house can't be a republic in a Federal nation.

C.O
And?

COLONEL
He now calls it Kalakuta Empire. He is still the Black President. And the Chief Priest of the African Shrine.

COMMANDING OFFICER
And what does that mean?

SCENE 26, ACT 1

Shot on fela in bandages and P.O.P

FELA

Obasanjo is an incipient sadist. And he will hear more from me. This 'mumu' burnt my house, Threw my mother through the window. Beat up everyone in my house including my brother, Beko. I am going to give him a gift for his wrong. In Africa, if a coffin is presented to a living that means, he don finish for am. Obasanjo is going to get his own coffin. I will personally deliver it to him at Dodan Barracks.

LAWYER

Fela, just get your act together. The people are waiting to hear from you.

FELA

Lawyer, you self run that time.

LAWYER

I have never seen such lawlessness

FELA

The law is an ass! Unknown soldier? That was a battalion from Abalti Barracks. T.Y Danjuma ordered the "ZOMBIES'

LAWYER

Fela, you were going to be killed. That was the order

FELA

You know I no dey run from dem. But that day I engaged my feet in rapid discussion. 'Mo ba ese mi soro'.

LAWYER

The Decca people are not paying. We need all the money we can get. You can't even perform again. Not even at the shrine.

FELA

Leave Decca. I am going to swoop on their premises and live there until they pay me. That's African. Like your people, osomaalo gbowo mi loni.

LAWYER

The white boy there will shit in his pants when he see you. Pass me the lighter.

Lighter is passed into Lawyer, lights it. Flame came on screen.

SCENE 27, ACT 1

At Decca's premises sitting at M.D.s desk

Shot on Fela sitting at the reception

FELA

My name is Fela Anikulapo Kuti. I have death in my pouch. I have refused to die. All the beatings I get from police and soldier were meant to kill me. But I have survived it. I do not subscribe to white names. I am an African proper. Fela Anikulatpo- Kuti- you see this letter written by MKO Abiola that I am a trouble-maker musician. He says there that my music is reactionary and that I incite the people against government. So therefore, my royalties should not be paid for seven albums. Even my own money the whiteman and MKO Abiola, government thief, are now stealing my money.

Gets up

That is why I am here. I am not leaving this place until I get my money, I don't have house. I can't perform. So how do I feed. I have to go after those owning me. So DECCA, give me my money. No unnecessary begging.

In the Recording Studio Interior Fela leaves studio, Inside M.D's officer sitting on edge of table

82

FELA

I don complete our 7 album contract. And you never pay one kobo.

M.D

Fela, your music is unpopular. Nobody is buying. I have the financial records to show for it.

FELA

He be like say 'ori e o pe' dey worry you. My music is unpopular? God punish you. Come to the Shrine and see for yourself. Your grand father!

M.D.

Please be gentlemanly. Your political view is not my concern. I am a business man.

FELA

Abi you wan make I craze for here? *(Fela gets up pulls down cabinet and scared the hell out of M.D)*

M.D.

Please be calm. You can't understand. I believe you are a gentleman

FELA

I no be gentleman at all, at all. Just give me my money I am not leaving this place

M.D.

Please, take it easy

FELA

Oro ebe o sele Give me my money. You chop wintch?.

SCENE 28, ACT II

OBEY

Fela, this is not begging. I will personally see that you're paid in full. Baawa We are all from the same source including Obasanjo. Baawa

FELA

That is why they should wicked me. Even my mother. And Beko. And other people living in the area. You sef don show me before. You stole my number one dancer, Dele. Look, you people are crazy.

SCENE 29, ACT 1

SHOT ON THE DEFENCE, HQ
VOICE
Call me Major Majekodunmi

ANOTHER VOICE
Yes sir,

Shot on commanders officer. Major Majekodunmi marches in. On Attention as he reach Commanders desk

MAJOR MAJEKODUNMI
Morning sir!

COMMANDER
I have the Anya report on Kalakuta. It didn't say your father owns the property. So, your father is the King of Boys. That is a gentleman. Unlike this rascal. I am sure, you are glad we kicked him out. Anyway, the King of Boy's can't have his house back. If he really wants it, he should go to court. The Federal Government has acquired it and the surrounding lands. The purpose of which will be announced later.

Ehh, you understand what I mean. Fela and your Dad have one thing in common. They celebrate perpetual youth. Don't we all have the child in us, Peter Pan. Major!

MAJEKODUNMI

Yes sir,

COMMANDER

No victor. No vanquished 'Ojoro' cancelled.

SCENE 30, ACT 9

CROSS ROAD HOTEL, YABA

Hotel room with friends and sympathizers. Long shot of Fela with company.

FELA

You all see what this military governments have come to. They burnt my house. And I can't even work. The two judges at the inquiry cannot see the criminality of all these. Their report says one "unknown soldier" did it. That was a battalion from Abalti. General Danjuma ordered the assault on my house. How can you do this to a citizen?

JK BRIMAH

This is a very bad government. Military governments are the worse thing to ever happen in the African continent. Their sole purpose is to destroy and loot. In their barracks, they share the spoils of war. It has always been a military tradition, destroy, kill and loot.

OSOBU

Military government are unlawful. They do not have the support of the people. Military apologists and career politicians have cornered this country into their pockets.

FELA

Wetin M.D Yusuf talk?

OSOBU

He was sympathetic. You know he is police. Soldiers control police. Police are handicap in a military government. They can't enforce the law; soldiers are above the law by decree. They make the law. Can you imagine? They march in, then create a breakdown of law and order.

FELA

Is this not a breakdown of law and order? Where is the civility in this "rogbodiyan". This is a confusion. They stole my money and raped the girls.

OSOBU

Fela, what about that girl? The soldier's daughter.

FELA

Leave her for me.

JK BRIMA

I think I saw her few minute ago. But, Fela are you going ahead with your plans for the girls.

FELA

Yes, now. I am African. And it will put the girls in good stead. All these name callings will stop.

OSOBU

I know you will save them from further derogatory remarks at last. They will all have a sense of belonging.

FELA

Equal partners in progress. They have been through thick and thin with me. They deserve more.

SCENE 31, ACT 1

Shot on an outside rally of Young African Pioneers. Placard and all Camera pan through crowd as Fela speaks.

FELA

Brothers and sisters. Look around you. What do you see? Homelessness, Hunger. Injustice. Corruption. Criminal display of stolen money from the national treasury. Ordinary safe drinking water, you cannot get it. Electricity has been replaced by candles and lantern caused by government incompetence, maladministration, nepotism, favoritism and pen robbery.

And when they catch the small thief, it is death by firing squad. What about dem? Ten months in jail.

Close up shot on Fela
Young African Pioneers, we have to take up arms against these crooks. We are not going to use guns and bullets. We are going to use music. Music is the weapon of the future.
We are going to create awareness for Blackism; a force of the mind. The African Personality will inculcate that Africaness that will reject all colomentality. Reject, refuse and eradicate every form of second slavery. Africa is the FUTURE: We have been a world power. Again, we will be a world power. We shall not be slaves again. Never again will Africa be a doormat for the whiteman. Go and read African history. The atrocities and subversive imposition on Africa is dehumanizing. But we have survived the abuse. Now is the

97

time to fight for the future of AFRICA. See what their foreign companies do. All the profit they make with our cheap labour, they carry our money go despite the yeye product and service they give us to buy. YOUNG AFRICAN PIONEERS fight back. Mobilize against second slavery. They are destroying our economy; so we can come to their country and do menial and cheap labour which their citizen cannot do. You might think the airplane is better than the slave ship, my brother, when cold catch you, you go know say Africa better. The black man is an invincible man. He is an endangered specie in their country.

Shot of KKK in white bedsheet hanging a black man
They systematically kill more black men every year than anywhere else. The Blackman is a strange fruit. Our leaders are so dunce they don't understand the situation. That means they don't have sense wiseness. Common sense is different from inner sense 'ogbon inu', belle sense.

Young African Pioneer, Nkwame Nkrumah says, identify and define yourself!

SCENE 32, ACT 1

Midday, Bright and Sunny
Shot on coffin carried shoulder high singing hit track, "ZOMBIE" on street. Fela and entourage.

FELA
Olusegun Obasanjo, Shehu Yar' adua o di gbere o,

CHORUS
Yeeparipa o, Yeeparipa o, Yeeparipa o o o
Yeeparipa, Yeeparipa, Yeeparipa o

Crowd moves along barrack fence

FELA
Obasanjo o di gbere ni yen

CHORUS
Yeeparipa yepa
Yeeparipa yepa Yeeparipa yepa Yeeparipa yepa o

At Gate. Soldiers tries to stop possession assault. Fela finally throws coffin as it slides into Dodan Barracks

...Dem no won take am
Yes, dem take am
Who go won take coffin
Na di bad bad bad things wey dem do...

SCENE 33, ACT I

Fela and entourage disperse in a bus Speeds · off. At marriage gathering. Fela sits with girls in beads and wrapper awaiting marriage vows. Officiating Ifa Priest joins Fela and girls in traditional wedlock. Together at group photograph flash. Shot freezes.

SCENE 33, ACT II

Long location

Shot of airport MMIA Lagos Fela is seen at custom desk.

CUSTOM

Fela, you are carrying more money than the government stipulates. Do you know you have committed an offence against the FOREX regulation bonded by decree.

FELA

Frowning at custom officer

Close up on Fela

Look, my brother, this money is for the 77 members of my band. It is not even enough as stipulated for each person. Officially, this is just for 5 members. We have sixteen concert tour of America. You're intimidating me.

CUSTOM

Shot of uniformer, stripes and all

I have to arrest you. You have contravened the decree. Fela Anikulapo Kuti. You're under arrest. Find me something. I go release you.

FELA

Fela's wives are now gathered
Find you something?
Are you sure of what you are saying? Look at all my band, if each person should hold their own FOREX. It will only reach 5.

CUSTOM

Please come with me. You have to write a statement.
Shot on screen

Shot on Screen
Fela was tried and jailed 5 years for possession of excess foreign currency by a military tribunal of the Buhari/Idiagbon military junta. The presiding Judge, Okoro-Odogwu on a jury tour of the prison, he met FELA in his hospital sick bed. In his piety, the Judge apologized for his harsh judgment. "My hands were tied. I am sorry". The military government of Babangida tampered justice with mercy. Fela Anikulapo-Kuti was released after 3 ½ years.

SCENE 34, ACT 1

In his house Gbemisola Street, Ileja, Lagos. A Press Conference of some sort. Camera flash etc.

FELA

The judge don beg me. My brother, he say make I no vex.

REPORTER

Are you going to sing about prison life?

FELA

Close up shot

No. my music has changed. I am going to put a more African introduction into it. There will be a big conga drum and another bass guitar. The only band in the world that use two bass guitars.

REPORTER

Do you have any admiration for this is military government on your release?

FELA

Head shot of Fela

The whole thing is spiritual, Babangida is a spirit. But I operate from a higher plane. I am on the 9th plane. I am now an evolved person. I an no longer human. I' am "Abami Eda". A strange one. Everything that happened to me is in the Ifa oracle.

REPORTER

You are not making yourself clear? Are you not FELA again.

FELA

I still be FELA. I be 'Abami Eda'. Look, reporter you are disturbing me. I have not seen my people in 3 ½ years.

REPORT

What do you miss most?

FELA

I miss women and smoking. That's what you want to hear.

REPORTER

Has the press become your enemy so soon?

FELA

Shot on Fela
I will never touch a newspaper and money, lailai. You were part of the problem. You glorified mediocrity when you should be condemning power abuse, oppression and injustice.

WOMAN REPORTER

Are we going to see a fiery Fela singing a more militant songs?

FELA

My music will now spiritualize your senses. It is going to be heavy. Come to the Shrine. You will hear authentic African spirituals from the spirit world. It is going to explore the minds of man inhumanity to man.

Scene 35, ACT 1

DAY

In Fela's House. Rowdy and milling around.
Shot on Beko staring at Fela from above the rim of his glasses

BEKO

We can't take this lying low. This country continued to dismember every citizen. I have to take up advocacy.

FELA

Beko, everything has a reason. It is spiritual. I know you only believe in cause and effect. You are rational. I am not. I see thing as revealed by ancestral spirit.

BEKO

I have concluded to fight this system of organized government by arrangement; that keeps recycling itself. The people are worst to show for it.

ENTER JKB

JKB

Beko, the smooth operator, you are beginning to sound louder, now. Don't you see all the nonsense things around you?

FELA

They cannot provide safe drinking water, no electricity. The people don't have homes. No house is a home. No security. No sense of belonging. The people are alienated in the scheme of things. No justice, no security for lives and properties.

Can somebody tell me what the fuck is going on?

E be like say I wan craze.

BEKO

Are you sure you are the only one going crazy? I don't see any sane person in this country anymore.

JKB

There are no real men anymore. What we have left are inadequate husband, ill-equipped fathers and uncommitted men. 'Ko si okunrin meta mo'.

FELA

These leaders in Africa are just blind to the needs of the people. They are short sighted and lacked the visions of great Africans leaders who they have either edged out of power or killed innocently with the help of Europe and America who don't want an emerging Africa. I never knew a government of my country can come burning my house, claiming the land and jailing me for sabotaging the economy. It just dawn on me that the social impact of my music is making them uncomfortable. After dem hear 'pansa pansa', dem go hear, wen!

SCENE 35 ACT II

Night

ROBBERY SCENE

On Bridge shot on Fela sitting beside driver. It is night. He is smoking. (first and only time in the script) A robbery is going on.

To one of the girls

FELA

Never reach for una make we hear word. Abi?

1ST GIRL

I dey warn you. You dey do pass yourself. If na you nko? you go gree? Why be say na my own you put yansh. Abi you wan tell me say na you sabi Fela pass everybody.

2ND GIRL

For your pocket! My own be say anytime I wan see Fela, I must see am. Na in dey gree for me. (Sound of sporadic shooting)

FELA

Soon as gangs get to Fela. On recognition, order summoning others. All gathered creating a wall.
Dis 'ogbologbo' dey operate (Fela, calm, looks out into the lagoon).

1ST ROBBER
Hey, na Fela! Na Fela! Fela!

2ND ROBBER
Black President! Abami Eda!

1ST ROBBER
Clear Road! Baba 70! Eleniyan! The Chief Priest!

1ST ROBBER
(Order pull out of Fela's vehicle) cleer jagajaga for road! Fela dey come .

FELA
In clenched fist salute. Easy, Easy (All robbers at an attention)

1ST ROBBER
(All set in Possession) Give 100 gun salute for Fela the Black President! (Gun salute) Onile Orisa! (Sporadic gunshots) elewele!

FELA
Make una come Shrine *(gives out wraps of NNG to robbers)*

SCENE 36, ACT 1

NIGHT SATURDAY COMPREHENSIVE SHOW

FELA throws kolanut divinations. Shirtless. Painted face. Perform rites in the shine. Pulls cockerels neck, splatters blood on deities. Serves communion.

FELA

Allah wakba na shit!
Allah wakba na mother fucker!
Jesus Christ im senior broda.
Halleluu!

Chorus:
Halleluoya!

Camera focus on two books burning.

SCENE 37, ACT 1

INTERIOR FELA'S LIVING ROOM
Fela sit on chair. Feet up Smoking, watching TV. Shot on door as it opens, personal assistant comes in

SHOT ON Keji Ade-Hamilton. Surrounded by residents as they feel his new look
PERSONAL ASSISTANT
Fela, na Keji. He don come, e don change true-true
Shot Back At Fela's living room. Keji sits

FELA
Shot on a surprised Fela
Hey, see you. Na you fine like dis

KEJI
Shots move to Fela / Keji
I be new person now. I am on the outside.

FELA
You don stop all that nonsense heroine and cocaine. You know say dat na the problem wey I get with you. You were good. Great talent. Na that thing. You know I can't stand it. You are like a son to me.

KEJI
Thank you. I am a changed person. No more of that in my life. I am clean as a newborn baby

FELA
Dem say you don be Pastor

KEJI
Na true. I have my own anti-drug non-governmental organization. I now campaign against use and abuse of drugs.

FELA
That's wonderful. If that's what Jesus Christ did to you. Then I like Him. Whatever you need to champion your cause, I will be very glad to assist.

SCENE 37, ACT II

SHOT BACK ON KEJI

KEJI
I want start off my campaign against drugs, I want your permit to start this anti-drug campaign from the Shrine.

FELA
Hey Keji, you know you can have it.

SCENE 38, ACT I

DAY: M. D. Yusuff house.

M. D. YUSSUF

Holding Out Wrapped Package .Sitting in his gazebo.
Fela girls enjoying the surrounding

Haa, what do we have here?

FELA

It's a gift for you. You are a light of truth

M.D YUSUFF

Shot on M.D
I really appreciate it. Fela, I admire your courage. Especially your fighting spirit.
It's true, the military have destroyed our psyche. We now have a breakdown of law and order. They don't like your political correctness.

FELA

Camera pan to Fela
They should go back to their barracks. In the outskirt of town. After town

M.D. YUSUFF

Close up M.D

Your cousin, Wole, had similar brushes with them. The power abuse and oppressive governance disgust him. He wanted to go through Idiroko then. They won't let him. I had to let him loose. It's a bad situation now to be Nigerian. It's not easy.

I'll come look you up . But they say you don't have toilet in the shrine.

FELA

Close up on Fela

Shit never catch you!

M.D. YUSSUF

Fela, do you believe in God?

FELA

Close shot

I believe in the spiritual of an higher force, 'Olodumare' whose power cord I connect with my ancestral spirit.

M.D. YUSSUF

Looking at camera

Fela was betrayed by the moral hypocrisy of this injurious and coercive country. And I was part of it.

Fela Anikulapo-Kuti was a cure to our diseased society.

SCENE 38, ACT II

DAY INTERIOR AFRICAN SHRINE

Shot on Keji. Camera pans to Shrine guest smoking and drinking.
KEJI
Cocaine will mess up your life. Heroine will destroy you, Marijuana will mar your future. Come to Jesus Christ. He will take you to the path of righteousness. He is the only way. He is the truth and the light. The truth shall set you free. Don't live with the illusion of drugs. It will only take you away from the belief in yourself. I am a living example. I am free and saved from the clutches of the devil I am free.
Thank God, I am free. Halleluyah, thank you Jesus, I am free at last!

O happy day
O happy day
When Jesus wash my sins away
Cap in hand. Keji take offerings.

SCENE 39, ACT I

Location shot
DAY: In Fela's Gbemisola house. Living room

4TH PRESS
Can you categorize your music? And your earlier influence?

FELA
Close up shot
I play African Music. Afrobeat was a definition. I love John Coltrane, Miles Davies, Charlie Parker was good. Kofi Ghanaba /Guy Warren was good, too. I am more inclined to traditional music from the villages.

My music is a vehicle for development; a means of communicating new ideas and information to the people towards achieving national development and personal growth.

My music basically is to mobilize the people for socio-political awareness and emancipation.

Where the electronic and print media cannot reach, my music aim for self development, actualization and empowerment.

SCENE 40, ACT I

Shot of the Threatre Arts Hall at the university of It is a tete-a-tete. Sitted across table facing each other. Camera from each others eye view.

FELA

African renaissance is now. There is no two way about it. First, we have to free our mind from the white man value system.

ESI KINNI

What about our homes and school? We teach unAfrican ways of live. We emphasize the virtues of the whiteman. We disrespect our culture and tradition, we also belittle whatever comes out of the continent.

FELA

We have to start appreciating ourselves. Teach the right history. Promote our cultural heritage. There must be emphasis on the whiteman's intention. These privatization and globalization are just to bamboozle the people. Most important, is the whiteman's determination to keep Africa down for their market.

ESI KINNI

To accept their standard and value system, is to disorient us.

FELA

All traditional industries in Africa have been abandoned in the villages.
That is where you can still see some elements of our Africaness.

ESI KINNI

The city dwellers are fast loosing grips on what's of left our being as an African. They don't appreciate traditional music. They love fast food and fancy restaurants. They wear cloths with someone else names written on them. You should see and read all the nonsense from the obscene to the derogatory, Africans now wear about. "Your face or mine" 'Girls do it better'.

FELA

One boy came to the shrine wearing "HOMEBOY" I told him is an houseboy.

ESI KINNI

House nigger! Even the boys wear perm and curly hairs.

FELA

I don't let them come to the shrine. I kick them out. What's better than a nice afro or a cornrow weave.

ESI KINNI

Our women make me sick. Despite all the side effects of bleaching, some still do it and they smell too. I really like your song, "Yellow Fever". It is good awareness but our government are just indifferent.

FELA

They are guilty as hell. They are false. So they embrace falsification. How can you change the colour of your skin. That is why our government, too take dictations, advice, from Europe and America. They should evolve the traditional governing system. Kwame Nkrumah embraced it. Ghana is better off for it now.

ESI KINNI

I like you. You never give up. They get the jitters when you talk. The press should get your opinion all the time.

FELA

The press can be hypocritical. They do because, government sweep on them. They want to save their head.
I have been to jail, Police custody, arrested, assaulted, battered, kicked out of my house, burnt, killed my mama, taken over as government property. I was practically homeless and forbidden to sing and make a living in my own country. Can you imagine such mental agony?

ESI KINNI

You are strong. You survived. You are not ordinary. The ancestors of Africa are your guiding spirit, Abami Eda. Ordinarily, you would have broken down. Probably, in a crazy house now.

FELA

I will still fight them till I breath my last.

ESI KINNI

You are a fighter. Don't ever give up on the struggle. It is your mission

FELA

The struggle must stop. Africa will be free. Every conspiracy to enslave Africa again has failed. It is a revelation from the ancestors. All these money making organization and multi nationals are slave drivers.

Their plans will never happen, lai lai, e no go happen. Africa will be free. There is no amount of historical distortion, manipulation and lies that can keep AFRICA down.

Africa will emerge from this obscurity. All Africans all over the world are set to raise Africa from its present state. They know the white man in and out. All those foolish leaders will be kicked out with their insolent subordinates. A new Africa will emerge. The world will bow at our perseverance and strength to withstand all the abuse, degradation, opposition and suppression. The fight has begun. Black people all over the world are set to Africa. It will be an intellectual revolution.

No guns. No bullets.

Fela facing camera
Africa is the center of the world, check your world map and see. There is a reason for occupying that vantage position.

We have survived slavery, the scramble and partition, the 'yeye' independence. We will renew the African Personality, for African Unity. Afrika will evolve! When e reach 'karangida' una go see!

SCENE 40, ACT II

Fela is sitted alone in a room before a large imposing table. And NDLEA logo stares at every angle.

Fela clears throat in usual manner. Has been in detention for a couple of days.

1ST VOICE

Before we charge am, I don't shut in big mouth for am.
Him think say na 'moinmoin' matter. No be 'Akara' at all.

2ND VOICE

Let's go interrogate the accuse
I have never met the man
He might give us an added value to this our campaign Though he can be sarcastic.

1ST VOICE

Person wey dey smoke Indian Hemp?

NIGHT

Fela is sitting on a chair. Handcuffed and manacled.
He remains unbowed. A long table with 4 empty chairs faces camera.
Woman in / trouser suit walks in sit on table edge.

WOMAN

Mr. Fela Anikulapo- Kuti, you have refused to write a statement. You want to see your lawyer?

FELA

I'm not Mister. I am a Master I don't need to see my lawyer. My lawyer wants to see me. You want me to state that you harassed me in my house and destabilize my household, my family?

WOMAN

I was not in your house and where do you live?

FELA

My house

WOMAN

I mean the address.

MAN

Officer, what are you saying to this man?

WOMAN

I'm trying to get him to write a statement

FELA

Say wetin happen? I thief or I kill person. Dem say I rape woman? What kind of country is this? you can't even have fun, enjoy yourself in your own house. Na wa o. no wonder this country is fucked!

Supposing person come your house say why you dey do wetin you dey do for enjoyment? Will you tell him 'abeg sir'

WOMAN (CONTD)

In your house, there are under age girls living with you. That's abduction. Some are confirmed pregnant and there are the free use of substances believed to be marijuana, Indian hemp.

FELA
See, I don't know about Indian what I smoke is cigarette and Nigerian Natural Grass (NNG). Grown here in Obiaruku. I used it for creativity and an afrodisiac, it is very good for fucking.

WOMAN
You 'll have to mind your language. You are in the custody of the NDLEA.

FELA
Mind my language? You handcuffed me, manacled my feet and you expect me to talk in a civil manner while you are treating me like a beast of no nation, a common criminal?

2ND OFFICER
Fela, be careful of what you wish for Africa. You pure intention behind this Africanism vision of a new Africa is paving way for the unimaginable nightmare you are going through. Can't you just quit and sing your music for entertainment?

1ST OFFICER
You look so sickly. You are dying.

VUW
What happens to a dead composer anyway? He decomposes. You music is degenerate. Vulgar.

FELA

Come Shrine and listen to my new compositions?

FELA

CLOSE UP SHOT

So, na Gestapo una dey now. Na to come person house come drag come NDLEA say, he smoke Igbo. Na criminal offence for person to dey fuck in wife for in own house. Una dey vex me. No be small.

Men com in: an army General (3 star, mustached)

GENERAL

Shege! Danboro Barka. Hmm na im be dis?

(Looks menacingly at Fela)
You dey sing say soja government bad. Now soja don catch you.
You dey smoke cocaine and heroine?

FELA

I don't touch that stuff.

GENERAL

You dey sing say water no dey, house no dey, light no dey, food no dey, work no dey. Which one concern you, sef.
FELA ANIKULAPO-KUTI JOINED THE ANCESTRAL SPIRIT ON AUGUST 7, 1997 AFTER THE ASSAULT AND ARREST IN HIS GBEMISOLA STREET RESIDENCE,

LAGOS, NIGERIA. THE AFRICAN SHRINE WAS SEALED UP BY MEN OF THE GENERAL BAMANIYI'S, NDLEA. THIS ASSAULT AND HARASSMENT COST FELA THE EGYPT 80 A SCHEDULED 16 NATION CONCERT TOUR OF EUROPE.
AFRICA WILL BE FREE. All form of Europe and American Influences should be rejected. All stooge African leaders will wither or be cut down like grass.

SCENE 41, ACT I
DAY: Student Classroom SCENE
Sitting in their desk .A discussion of another kind goes on

1ST Student
Politically, we should integrate with countries that are either similar or compatible.

2ND Student
Camera pan through
Africa is too diverse for one government. It is a good concept but there's a clear difference in opinion over intensity of integration. We have to slow down to let it mature.

3RD Student
You know the problems involved that they had in the European union with 25 members now 27, to arrive at the common position, we have to have 53.

1ST Student
It is clear, there will be problems involved for people to adjust, I believe that the 53 states will find a way of sharing and joining in the concensus to the direction of our continental economy.

3RD Student
African unity is vital to make the continent truly independent of the West.

2ND Student

There is need to establish a single government, foreign policy and army.

1ST Student

The question of unity of African states is absolutely necessary. The key issue is to attain it.

3RD Student

Close up shot
We have to start now, to move towards a new country-Africa

.

1ST Student

We should be ready to abandon partially or totally our sovereignty to join a United African Government. We should have no problem. Every President ought to sign the Pan Africa agreement.

2ND Student

A small group of states should sign up now towards a federation of African states for others to follow. We had a Senegambia. And there is ECOWAS. African Union has only been a talk-talk thing. Nothing concrete has been achieved.

3RD Student

I believe African interest would be best served through economic and political integration. We must adopt a bottom-up approach. I believe that such integration should be gradual.

2ND Student

There's need for a gradual approach to strengthen the existing regional nations. It is better than signing away each other's sovereignty.

SCENE 42 ACT II

NIGHT: A round table meeting

NANA (Female)
Africa is a nuclear free zone; no nuclear warhead on African soil.

KAUNDA
THE Pelindaba treaty declares Africa free from nuclear warheads and weapons.

CAMARA
This is a challage for an African High command according to Kwame Nkrumah. We have to resist the arabization of Africa by Gadaffi

KOFI
The United States AFRICOM is a threat of aggression against Africa, so also is the Ghadaffi initiative. And the Chinese, too in Sudan?

FANTA
We should all resist Western initiatives. Now the United States is eyeing Somalia. The apartheid in Sudan must stop. There must be a majority rule. The war in Darfur is aggression against black people. Bashir should be tried for genocide.

We will not allow the U.S. AFRICOM in Africa! This is a challenge for all African leaders.

AKIN
Following the experiences of IRAN, IRAQ and AFGHANISTAN, many African leaders views the United State Proposal as a ploy to colonize, and ....

CAMARA
.... And militarize the continent!

SHORT BREAK